D0519076

thelittlebookof...
Cocktails

thelittlebookof...
Cocktails

$$p$$

This is a Parragon Book

First published in 2005

Parragon
Queen Street House
4 Queen Street
Bath BA1 1HE, UK

Copyright © Parragon 2005

Photography by Steve Moss, Chris Linton, Roddy
Paine, Calvey Taylor-Haw, Pinpoint
Text complied by Alex Barker
Designed by Talking Design

Hardback ISBN 1-40546-123-3
Paperback ISBN 1-40546-124-1

Printed in China

Recipes containing raw eggs are not suitable for
children, convalescents, the elderly or pregnant
women. Please consume alcohol sensibly.

Contents

introduction to cocktails

The coolest and the classiest drinks around, cocktails are an invitation to combine fun and creativity with the glamour of the racy 1920s and 1930s. In the newest bar or the most traditional, you're never out of style asking for the all-time classic cocktail – a dry Martini. Drop into London's Savoy or Manhattan's Algonquin Hotel and try it.

Sit and watch the bartender perform – the fast action and easy chat, the smooth sharp shake, the perfect balance of flavours created with effortless speed, the finishing touches and flourishes that make you think he has invented this drink especially for you! And yet this is only a drink. You may find yourself thinking that maybe you could do that too, in the comfort of your own home?

That's just what this book is all about – giving you a wide and imaginative collection of cocktails – classic and contemporary – to suit every occasion and every taste. They are described simply and beautifully photographed, so you'll know exactly how to recreate and present them. Making cocktails is great fun, both for you and for your appreciative guests.

Cocktails made easy

There's no incomprehensible magic involved in mixing the perfect cocktail. It's a simple matter of combining the prescribed ingredients, at the perfect temperature and in the right order, and then serving the delicious result in the correct glass with a little flair. This little book tells you precisely how to do all that and shows you how the finished cocktail should look, and it's that easy. You don't even need any complicated equipment, although a blender and a shaker, as well as a wide selection of glasses, are fairly essential.

The Little Book of Cocktails is divided into five sections - classic, fruity, bubbly, shooters and non-alcoholic – and in each section you will find a cocktail with the character and the style to suit any occasion.

Classic cocktails There are literally thousands of different cocktails that have been created, celebrated and named, but only a handful have achieved classic status. Most of these owe their fame to the simplicity of their ingredients and the surprising complexity of their flavours. They also bask in the glamour of a bygone age, and their very names – from the Martini to the Harvey Wallbanger – conjure up images of big bands and ball gowns, movie stars and millionaires. Now you can capture the elegance of these classy drinks in just a matter of minutes. Here's looking at you, kid.

Fruity cocktails All the cocktails in this section have a base of fresh fruit juice or puréed fruit, and all keep that fruity flavour at the fore. From the tart freshness of grapefruit juice to the sweet smoothness of blended mango, these recipes are summer specials.

Bubbly cocktails Based on champagne, sparkling wine, cider and a variety of other bubbly drinks, these cocktails bring a celebratory touch to any occasion. This is the place to search for a glamorous or sexy champagne cocktail, or an unusual yet economical sparkling summer punch for the weekend barbecue.

Shooters These are short cocktails consisting of a mix of neat spirits, sometimes with ice or additional flavouring, but not greatly diluted with non-alcoholic ingredients. Some are intended to be knocked back in one, while others should be savoured, but all of them should be treated with respect, given their alcoholic strength.

Non-alcoholic While cocktails are colourful, festive and delicious, not everyone wants alcoholic drinks, even at a party. This chapter on non-alcoholic cocktails provides the answer to this dilemma: drinks with a sophisticated edge and adult appeal. Perfect for family occasions when youngsters wish to drink the same cocktails as the adults, or for those on driving duties.

Have fun making these cocktails. All the recipes are easy to follow – the only difficulty you may have will be in deciding which one to try first!

classiccocktails

If you've ever wondered how to make a
Bloody Mary or a Cosmopolitan then look
no further! This section will show you
how simple and easy it is to create a
wide variety of classic cocktails in your
own home.

zombie

The individual ingredients of this cocktail, including liqueurs and fruit juices, vary considerably from one recipe to another, but all Zombies contain a mixture of white, golden and dark rum in varying proportions.

Serves : 1

crushed ice cubes
2 measures dark rum
2 measures white rum
1 measure golden rum
1 measure Triple Sec
1 measure lime juice
1 measure orange juice
1 measure pineapple juice

1 measure guava juice
1 tbsp grenadine
1 tbsp orgeat
1 tsp Pernod
sprigs of fresh mint and
    pineapple wedges

1 Put crushed ice in a blender with all but the mint and pineapple.

2 Blend until smooth.

3 Pour, without straining, into a chilled Collins glass and dress with mint and a wedge of pineapple.

fuzzynavel

This is one of those cocktails with a name that plays on the ingredients – fuzzy to remind you that it contains peach schnapps and navel because it is mixed with orange juice.

Serves : 1
2 measures vodka
1 measure peach schnapps
250ml/8 fl oz orange juice
cracked ice cubes
physalis (cape gooseberry)

1 Shake the vodka, peach schnapps and orange juice vigorously over cracked ice until well frosted.
2 Strain into a chilled cocktail glass and dress with a physalis.

pinacolada

One of the younger generation of classics, this became popular during the cocktail revival of the 1980s and has remained so ever since.

Serves : 1
4–6 crushed ice cubes
2 measures white rum
1 measure dark rum
3 measures pineapple juice
2 measures coconut cream
pineapple wedges, to decorate

1 Whizz the crushed ice in a blender with the white rum, dark rum, pineapple juice and coconut cream until smooth.
2 Pour, without straining, into a tall chilled glass and dress with pineapple wedges.

tequilasunrise

This is one cocktail you shouldn't rush when making, or you will spoil the attractive sunrise effect produced by the grenadine slowly spreading through the orange juice.

Serves : 1
2 measures silver tequila
cracked ice cubes
orange juice
1 measure grenadine

1 Pour the tequila over cracked ice in a chilled highball glass and top up with the orange juice. Stir well to mix.

2 Slowly pour in the grenadine and serve with a straw.

tomcollins

This long cooling drink is a celebrated cocktail and was the inspiration for several generations of the Collins drinks family scattered around the globe.

Serves : 1
3 measures gin
2 measures lemon juice
½ measure sugar syrup
5–6 cracked ice cubes
soda water
slice of lemon

1 Shake the gin, lemon juice and sugar syrup vigorously over ice until well frosted.
2 Strain into a tall chilled tumbler and top up with soda water.
3 Dress with a slice of lemon.

longislandicedtea

Dating back to the days of the American Prohibition, when it was drunk out of cups in an attempt to fool the FBI that it was harmless, this cocktail has evolved from the original simple combination of vodka with a dash of cola!

Serves : 1

2 measures vodka

1 measure gin

1 measure white tequila

1 measure white rum

½ measure white crème de menthe

2 measures lemon juice

1 tsp sugar syrup

cracked ice cubes

cola

wedge of lime or lemon

1 Shake the vodka, gin, tequila, rum, crème de menthe, lemon juice and sugar syrup vigorously over ice until well frosted.

2 Strain into an ice-filled highball glass and top up with cola.

3 Dress with lime or lemon wedges.

screwdriver

Always use freshly squeezed orange juice to make this refreshing cocktail – it is just not the same with bottled juice. This simple, classic cocktail has given rise to numerous and increasingly elaborate variations.

Serves : 1
cracked ice cubes
2 measures vodka
orange juice
slice of orange

1 Fill a chilled glass with cracked ice cubes.
2 Pour the vodka over the ice and top up with orange juice.
3 Stir well to mix and dress with a slice of orange.

bloodymary

This classic cocktail was invented in 1921 at the legendary Harry's Bar in Paris. There are numerous versions – some much hotter and spicier. Ingredients may include horseradish sauce in addition to, or instead of, Tabasco sauce.

Serves : 1

dash Worcestershire
  sauce
dash Tabasco sauce
cracked ice cubes
2 measures vodka
splash dry sherry

6 measures tomato juice
juice of half a lemon
pinch celery salt
pinch cayenne pepper
celery stick with leaves
slice of lemon

1 Dash the Worcestershire sauce and Tabasco sauce over ice in shaker and add the vodka, splash of dry sherry, tomato juice and lemon juice.
2 Shake vigorously until frosted.
3 Strain into a tall chilled glass, add a pinch of celery salt and a pinch of cayenne and decorate with a celery stick and a slice of lemon.

pimm's no. 1

Pimm's No. 1 is a long, deliciously dry but fruity concoction, with a gin base flavoured with herbs. It was devised by James Pimm, a London restaurateur, in the late 19th century and was quite probably the original gin sling.

Serves : 1
ice
1 measure Pimm's No. 1
lemonade
strips of cucumber peel, sprigs of mint
  or borage
slices of orange and lemon

1 Fill a large chilled glass two-thirds full with ice and pour in the Pimm's.
2 Top up with lemonade and stir gently.
3 Dress with a twist of cucumber peel, a sprig of fresh mint and slices of orange and lemon.

singaporesling

In the days of the British Empire, the privileged would gather at their clubs in the relative cool of the evening and sip a Singapore Sling. Times may change, but it is still the ideal thirst-quencher on a hot summer's evening.

Serves : 1

2 measures gin
1 measure cherry brandy
1 measure lemon juice
1 tsp grenadine
cracked ice cubes
soda water
lime peel and cocktail cherries

1 Shake the gin, cherry brandy, lemon juice and grenadine vigorously over ice until well frosted.
2 Half fill a chilled highball glass with cracked ice cubes and strain in the cocktail.
3 Top up with soda water and dress with lime peel and cocktail cherries.

harveywallbanger

This well-known contemporary classic cocktail is a great party drink – mix it strong at first, then weaker as the evening goes by. Leave out the alcohol for drivers and no one will know!

Serves : 1
3 measures vodka
8 measures orange juice
2 tsp Galliano
ice cubes
cherry and slice of orange

1 Half fill a highball glass with ice, pour vodka and orange over the ice cubes and float Galliano on top.
2 Garnish with a cherry and slice of orange.
3 For a warming variant, mix a splash of ginger wine with the vodka and orange.

daiquiri

Daiquiri is a town in Cuba, where this drink was said to have been invented in the early part of the 20th century. A businessman had run out of imported gin and so had to make do with the local drink – rum – which, at that time, was often of unreliable quality.

Serves : 1

2 measures white rum
¾ measure lime juice
½ tsp sugar syrup
cracked ice

1 Pour the rum, lime juice and sugar syrup over ice and shake vigorously until well frosted.
2 Strain into a chilled cocktail glass.

cosmopolitan

This contemporary classic, made famous by the TV show 'Sex in the City', is the only drink to serve at a trendy party!

Serves : 1

2 measures vodka
1 measure Triple Sec
1 measure fresh lime juice
1 measure cranberry juice
orange peel

1 Shake all the ingredients over ice until well frosted.
2 Strain into a chilled cocktail glass.
3 Dress with a strip of orange peel.

buck's fizz

Invented at Buck's Club in London,
the original was invariably made with
Bollinger champagne and it is true that
the better the quality of the
champagne, the better the flavour.

Serves : 1
2 measures chilled fresh orange juice
2 measures champagne, chilled

1 Half fill a chilled flute with orange juice, then gently
    pour in the chilled champagne.

champagnecocktail

The classic champagne cocktail can be too sweet for some. It is the brandy that gives the treat and the kick, so you could leave out the sugar!

Serves : 1

1 sugar cube
2 dashes Angostura bitters
1 measure brandy
champagne, chilled

1 Place the sugar cube with the drops of bitters in the base of a chilled flute.
2 Pour on the brandy and top up slowly with champagne.

charleston

This little number combines several tastes and flavours to produce a very lively drink. Don't drink it when you are thirsty, you might want too many!

Serves : 1
¼ **measure gin**
¼ **measure dry vermouth**
¼ **measure sweet vermouth**
¼ **measure Cointreau**
¼ **measure kirsch**
¼ **measure maraschino**
ice and a twist of lemon

1 Shake all the ingredients except the lemon together well over ice and strain into a small chilled cocktail glass.

2 Dress with a twist of lemon.

moscowmule

This cocktail came about by lucky happenstance during the 1930s. An American bar owner had overstocked on ginger beer, and a representative of the soft drinks company invented the Moscow Mule to help him out.

Serves : 1

2 measures vodka
1 measure lime juice
cracked ice cubes
ginger beer
slice of lime

1 Shake the vodka and lime juice vigorously over ice until well frosted.
2 Half fill a chilled highball glass with cracked ice cubes and strain the cocktail over them.
3 Top up with ginger beer. Dress with a slice of lime.

kirroyale

A wicked improvement on the simple cassis and white wine drink.

Serves : 1
few drops cassis or to taste
½ measure brandy
champagne, chilled

1 Put the cassis and brandy into the base of a flute.
2 Top up with champagne to taste.

martini

For many, this is the ultimate cocktail. It is named after its inventor, Martini de Anna de Toggia, not the famous brand of vermouth!

Serves : 1
3 measures gin
1 tsp dry vermouth, or to taste
cracked ice cubes
green pitted olive

1 Pour the gin and vermouth over cracked ice in a mixing glass and stir well to mix.
2 Strain into a chilled cocktail glass and dress with a cocktail olive.

whitelady

Simple, elegant, subtle and much more powerful than appearance suggests, this is the perfect cocktail to serve before an al fresco summer dinner.

Serves : 1
2 measures gin
1 measure Triple Sec
1 measure lemon juice
cracked ice cubes

1 Shake the gin, Triple Sec and lemon juice vigorously over ice until well frosted.

2 Strain into a chilled cocktail glass.

fruitycocktails

Deliciously mouthwatering and temptingly
fruity, this collection of cocktails combines
your favourite spirits, liqueurs and wines
with a wide range of fruit juices and purées.
Have fun trying the different combinations!

seabreeze

Pink grapefruit juice is much sweeter
and subtler than its paler cousin, so it
is ideal to mix in cocktails where you
want just a slight sharpness.

Serves : 1
1½ measures vodka
½ measure cranberry juice
ice
pink grapefruit juice to taste

1 Shake the vodka and cranberry juice over ice until
frosted.
2 Pour into a chilled tumbler or long glass and top up
with grapefruit juice to taste.
3 Serve with a straw.

mississippifizz

This fizz is packed with fruity flavours
and a subtle taste of frozen gin.

Serves : 1
2 measures gin
1 measure fresh lime juice
1 measure passion fruit juice
¼ measure syrop de gomme
3 dashes orange flower water
1 measure soda water
crushed ice

1 Whizz all the ingredients together in a blender on
   fast for a few seconds or until really frothy.
2 Pour into a large iced cocktail glass or highball
   glass and serve with a straw.

trixiedixie

As there is lots of fruit and fruit juice
in this cocktail, you may not want to
add much soda water, just ice well and
offer soda water to taste.

Serves : 4

3 measures gin
6 measures Southern Comfort
3 measures lime juice
4 slices fresh pineapple
ice
soda water
sliced pineapple

1 Whizz the first four ingredients in the blender on slow
until creamed and frothy.
2 Pour into ice-filled glasses and top up with the soda
water to taste just before serving.
3 Dress with slices of pineapple.

seeingred

There is a real kick to this cocktail, and the cranberry juice imparts a wonderfully vivid colour.

Serves : 1
1 measure red vodka
1 measure peach schnapps
3 measures cranberry juice
crushed ice
soda water
frozen cranberries

1 Shake the first three ingredients over ice until well frosted.
2 Strain into a tall chilled cocktail glass, top up with soda water and float a few frozen cranberries on the top.

cinnamonpark

Cinnamon and other spices can make
all the difference to fruit-based
cocktails. Add to taste or sprinkle on
the top before drinking.

Serves : 1

1 measure vodka
2 measures pink grapefruit juice
½ measure Campari
1 dash syrop de gomme
pinch or two cinnamon
1 egg white
ice

1 Shake all the ingredients well over ice and strain
into a chilled medium-sized cocktail glass.

atomic

Deliciously flavoured with orange and mandarin, topped up with exotic fruit juices and decorated with kiwi, this eerie-looking drink tastes great.

Serves : 1
1¼ measures cognac
¾ measure Grand Marnier
¼ measure blue Curaçao
ice
3 measures exotic fruit juice
1 tsp fraise
kiwi slices

1 Shake the first three ingredients together over ice until frosted.
2 Strain into a chilled highball glass and top up with fruit juice.
3 Float in a few drops of fraise and dress with slices of kiwi.
4 Drink through a straw.

goldendawn

Like the sun rising over a tropical beach, the glow of the grenadine peeps through the brandy and orange.

Serves : 1
½ measure gin
½ measure Calvados
½ measure apricot brandy
½ measure mango juice
ice
dash grenadine

1 Mix the first four ingredients together over ice.
2 Strain into a cocktail glass and gradually add a dash of grenadine so the colour ripples through.

fruitcrazy

Melon and mango both have powerful flavours and perfumes, making this an exotic and delicious concoction.

Serves : 1

1 measure gin
½ measure melon liqueur
1 measure mango nectar
1 measure grapefruit juice
1 small egg white
ice cubes
slices of mango

1 Shake the first six ingredients together over ice until frosted.
2 Strain into a chilled long glass with more ice to top up and finish with a slice of mango.

rumcooler

The characteristic sweetness and
perfume of rum blends with so many
exotic fruits. You could try this with
mango and lychee.

Serves : 1
2 ice cubes
juice of 1 lime
1½ measures rum
1½ measures pineapple juice
1 medium-sized ripe banana, cut into chunks
lime peel

1 Whizz all the ingredients in a blender for about a
minute or until smooth.
2 Pour over ice into a chilled glass and finish with a
twist of peel.

yellowquiver

Two fruits mixed with three different
alcoholic drinks certainly makes for an
exciting cocktail – top it with a swirl of
blue Curaçao for a glamorous touch.

Serves : 1
½ measure Mandarine Napoleon
½ measure vodka
¼ measure Galliano
½ measure pineapple juice
¼ measure lemon juice
½ egg white
crushed ice
dash blue Curaçao

1 Shake all but the Curaçao over crushed iced until wel
frosted.
2 Pour into an iced cocktail glass and spoon the
Curaçao on top at the last moment.

kiwicrush

Made with plenty of crushed ice, this fruity combination quickly makes an adult slush. Enjoy before it goes past its best.

Serves : 1

2 measures light rum

½ measure melon liqueur

2 measures grapefruit juice

2 kiwi fruit, peeled

2 scoops crushed ice

1 Reserve a slice of kiwi.

2 Whizz all the remaining ingredients in a blender on a slow speed until slushy.

3 Pour into a large glass, finish with the slice of kiwi and drink through a straw.

yellowbird

This really is best made with a fresh, sweet, ripe pineapple, so you'll just have to make a jugful and invite some friends round to enjoy this treat.

Serves : 6
1 medium-sized ripe pineapple
3 measures dark rum
2 measures Triple Sec
2 measures Galliano
1 measure lime juice
ice cubes
pineapple leaves to finish

1 Blend the pineapple for 30 seconds in a processor, then add the next four ingredients and blend for another 10–20 seconds until smooth.

2 Pour into large cocktail glasses or tumblers filled with ice, and finish with pineapple leaves or a flower.

watermelon**man**

Watermelon is such a colourful and
tasty fruit that it makes a great mixer.
Don't be tempted to add more unless
you want to dilute the strength of your
cocktail.

Serves : 1
4 measures dry white wine
1 dash grenadine
4 cubes or chunks of watermelon
scoop crushed ice

1 Whizz all the ingredients together in a blender for
5–10 seconds until well frosted.
2 Pour into a tall glass and dress with a piece of melon
on a cocktail stick.

melonand**ginger**crush

A really refreshing summer drink, this melon crush is quick and simple to make. If you can't buy kaffir limes, ordinary limes are fine.

Serves : 4
1 melon, about 800g/1½lb
6 tbsp ginger wine
3 tbsp kaffir lime juice
crushed ice
1 lime

1 Peel, deseed and coarsely chop the melon flesh.
2 Place in a blender or food processor with the ginger wine and lime juice, and blend on high speed until the mixture is smooth.
3 Place plenty of crushed ice in 4 medium straight-sided glasses and pour the melon and ginger crush over the ice.
4 To add a decorative touch, cut the lime into thin slices, cut a slit in four of them and slip one onto the side of each glass. Add the remaining slices of lime to each glass.

on the vine

The wine you use in this cocktail can change the character of the mix totally. If you like a sweet drink, use a medium sweet or sweet wine. Otherwise, choose a dry or drier wine.

Serves : 1
½ measure apricot brandy
ice
dash grenadine
150ml/5 fl oz white wine or to taste
soda water
small bunch grapes

1 Stir the apricot brandy and ice in a large cocktail glass or wine goblet.
2 Add the grenadine and then pour on the wine.
3 Top up with soda for a longer, more refreshing drink.
4 Dress the glass with grapes.

birdofparadise

This is sometimes made with blue
Curaçao, but orange Curaçao gives a
much more appetising finishing colour.
However, it's up to you, so try them
both!

Serves : 1
1 measure gin, chilled
1 measure passion fruit nectar, chilled
½ measure orange Curaçao, chilled
crushed ice
1 thick slice watermelon – save a piece to decorate

1 Deseed the watermelon.
2 Blend all the ingredients together with the ice until
   partly frozen.
3 Pour into a tumbler or large cocktail glass and dress
   with a wedge of melon. You may need a spoon!

hightea

This variation on the classic Pimm's is a little stronger and bit more appley, yet still a great summer cocktail for special occasions.

Serves : 1
1 measure vodka
1 measure Pimm's No. 1
1 measure apple juice
ice
lemonade
cucumber strips and apple slices

1 Shake the first three ingredients over ice until frosted.
2 Strain into a chilled highball glass and top up with lemonade.
3 Finish with cucumber strips and apple slices.

adam'n'eve

Don't expect this cocktail to be full
of apples! The base is sharp and
astringent, while the top is sweet and
frothy – no discrimination here, of
course!

Serves : 1
2 measures Triple Sec
1 measure vodka
1 measure grapefruit juice
1 measure cranberry juice
ice
5–6 cubes pineapple
2 tsp caster sugar
crushed ice
strawberry

1 Shake the first four ingredients over ice until well
frosted.
2 Strain into a chilled long glass.
3 In a blender, whizz the pineapple with sugar and
1–2 tbsp of crushed ice to a frothy slush.
4 Float gently on the top of the cocktail.
5 Dress with a slice of strawberry.

bubblycocktails

The obvious choice for any celebration, bubbly cocktails are glamorous and indulgent. Don't limit yourself to champagne – try out the delicious concoctions using cider, wine and other sparkling drinks

montecarlo

The motor racing world always drinks champagne, especially in Monte Carlo, and this well-laced cocktail is definitely a Formula 1 special.

Serves : 1
½ measure gin
¼ measure lemon juice
ice
champagne or sparkling white wine
¼ measure crème de menthe
mint leaf

1 Stir the first two ingredients over ice until well chilled
2 Strain into chilled flutes and top up with champagne.
3 Finally drizzle the crème de menthe over the top and dress with a mint leaf.

ciderpunch

This may sound seriously strong but it isn't, and you can add more soda or ice to taste once the base is made.

Serves : 10
17 fl oz/500ml dry sparkling cider
5 fl oz/150ml cognac or brandy
5 fl oz/150ml Cointreau
ice
apple slices
10 fl oz/300ml soda water or dry ginger

1 Mix the first three ingredients together and chill in the refrigerator until required.
2 Pour into a large punch bowl with ice, apple slices and the soda water or dry ginger.
3 Serve in small cups or glasses.

theacrobat

Cider is not often used in cocktails, which is a pity as it is a great way to add length with a little strength to a drink.

Serves : 1
2 measures whisky
1 measure Cointreau
1 measure lime juice
ice
cider
piece of lime or lemon

1 Mix all the ingredients except cider over ice until frosted.
2 Strain into an ice-filled long glass.
3 Top up with cider and dress with a piece of lime or lemon.

long*tall*sally

A seriously strong champagne cocktail
with the perfume of herbs.

Serves : 1
¼ measure brandy
¼ measure dry vermouth
¼ measure Galliano
¼ measure mandarin liqueur
ice
champagne or sparkling wine

1 Stir the first four ingredients over ice and pour into
a tall chilled glass.
2 Top up with champagne.

shangri-la

This an excellent mix to liven up a not-so-exciting bottle of bubbly! It also makes an unusual mix for several people for a party.

Serves : 1
½ measure gin
¼ measure apricot brandy
½ measure orange juice
few drops grenadine
ice
Asti Spumante dry sparkling wine
slices of orange and lemon

1 Stir the first four ingredients with ice in a chilled highball or large wine glass.
2 Top up with sparkling wine and dress with fruit.

camparifizz

The bitter-sweet of Campari is a natural with orange juice and sparkling wine or champagne. You need very little Campari to add the distinctive colour and flavour.

Serves : 1

1 measure Campari
1 measure orange juice
crushed ice
champagne

1 Shake the first three ingredients together well until frosted and pour into a flute.
2 Top up with champagne.

orangesparkler

Serve this exotic version of a classic champagne cocktail for any occasion or simple celebration.

Serves : 1
⅔ **measure brandy**
⅓ **measure orange liqueur**
⅓ **measure lemon juice**
ice
Asti Spumante dry, iced

1 Shake the first three ingredients well together over ice.
2 Strain into a chilled champagne glass and top up with Asti Spumante to taste.

applefizz

Cider makes a great punch base, as it can be blended with many alcoholic drinks. This mix can't be made in advance, but it's easy to prepare for several people and then add more cider at the last minute to create extra fizz.

Serves : 1
150ml/5 fl oz sparkling cider or apple juice
1 measure Calvados
juice of half a lemon
1 tbsp egg white
generous pinch sugar
ice
slices of lemon and apple

1 Shake the first five ingredients together over ice and pour immediately into a highball glass (it may fizz up well).
2 Finish with a slice of lemon or apple or both. For more fizz at the last moment, top up with more cider.

mexicanfizz

The tart fruitiness of tequila is not often appreciated neat, but it is great with many of the sweetened and fuller flavoured mixers.

Serves : 1
2 measures tequila
½ measure grenadine
5–6 measures dry ginger ale
crushed ice

1 Shake the tequila, grenadine and half the ginger ale over ice until slushy and frosted.
2 Pour into a chilled tall glass and top up with more ginger ale to taste.
3 Drink through a straw.

ladyluck

The pear and apple flavours give a deep fruitiness to the final cocktail, so you could equally well use a sparkling white wine as the base.

Serves : 1
1 measure Calvados
1 measure pear nectar or ½ measure pear liqueur
slice of firm ripe pear
champagne, chilled

1 Pour the Calvados and pear nectar or liqueur into a chilled flute with a slice of pear.
2 Top up with chilled champagne.

tequilaslammer

A slammer is a fizzy version of a
shooter. The idea is that you pour the
ingredients directly into the glass,
without stirring. Then you cover the
glass with one hand to prevent spillage,
slam it down on the table to froth it
up, and drink the cocktail down in one!
Do ensure you use a strong glass!

Serves : 1

1 measure white tequila, chilled
1 measure lemon juice
sparkling wine, chilled

1 Put the tequila and lemon juice into a chilled glass.
2 Top up with sparkling wine.
3 Cover the glass with your hand and slam.
    Down in one.

bombaysherry**punch**

An unusual mix for a party, ideal to dilute as much as you wish.

Serves : 16
1 bottle brandy, chilled
1 bottle sherry, chilled
1 measure maraschino
1 measure Curaçao
2 bottles champagne or sparkling white wine, chilled
soda water, chilled
large ice cubes (set with fruit in them)
fruit to decorate

1 Mix the first four ingredients in a large punch bowl.
2 Add the wine and soda to taste and then add the fruit and ice cubes at the last minute.

sabrina

Perfect for lovers of sweet and fruity
cocktails, and the base is easy to
prepare in advance.

Serves : 1
½ measure gin
⅛ measure apricot brandy
½ measure fresh orange juice
1 tsp grenadine
¼ measure Cinzano
ice
sweet sparkling wine
orange and lemon slices

1 Shake the first five ingredients together
   over ice.
2 Pour into a tall glass and top up with sparkling wine.
3 Finish with slices of orange and lemon.

blacksparkler

Simply using sparkling water makes this a delicious summer party drink. If you wish to make it more celebratory, use sparkling white wine.

Serves : 1

1¾ measures cognac
¼ measure Crème de Mure
¼ measure lemon juice
1 tsp caster sugar
ice
soda water or sparkling white wine
frozen blackcurrants or berries

1 Shake the first four ingredients over ice until frosted.
2 Strain into a tall chilled cocktail glass and top up with soda water or wine.
3 Dress with fruit.

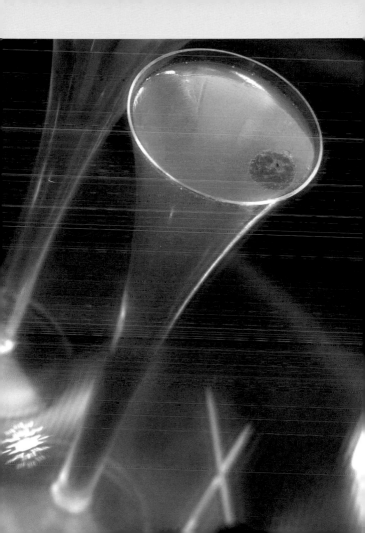

caribbeanchampagne

Both rum and bananas are naturally
associated with the Tropics, but wine
does not spring so readily to mind
when the Caribbean is mentioned.
However, remember that France
shares a long history with many of the
Caribbean islands, such as Martinique
and Guadeloupe.

Serves : 1
½ measure white rum
½ measure crème de banane
champagne, chilled
slice of banana, to decorate

1 Pour the rum and crème de banane into a chilled
flute.
2 Top up with champagne.
3 Stir gently to mix, and dress with a slice of banana.

shooters

Shooters are great as an after dinner tipple or for an entertaining evening spent with friends. But beware – the small size of these amazing-looking drinks certainly doesn't indicate a look of potency!

russiandouble

Vodka and schnapps are both very strong drinks, so handle with care!

Serves : 1
1 measure red vodka, iced
strips of lemon or orange peel
1 measure lemon vodka or schnapps, iced

1 Layer the drinks carefully in a chilled shot glass, putting a piece of peel in the first layer, and drink immediately.

hairofthedog

This well-known expression – a tot of whatever gave you the hangover in the first place – is in fact a popular Scottish 'morning after' tipple!

Serves : 1
1 measure Scotch whisky
1½ measures single cream
½ measure clear honey
ice

1 Gently mix the whisky, cream and honey together.
2 Pour into a cocktail glass over ice and serve with a straw.

tequilashot

According to custom this is the only way to drink neat tequila. It is often described as being smooth and tart, so adding lime juice and salt may sound contradictory, but it works!

Serves : 1
pinch salt
1 measure gold tequila
wedge of lime

1 Put the salt at the base of your thumb, between thumb and forefinger.
2 Hold the lime wedge in the same hand.
3 Hold the shot in the other hand.
4 Lick the salt, down the tequila and suck the lime.

auroraborealis

Like a pousse-café, this spectacular
coloured drink should not be mixed or
stirred. Leave it to swirl around the
glass, creating a multi-hued effect, and
try to detect the various flavours.

Serves : 1
1 measure iced grappa or vodka
1 measure iced green Chartreuse
½ measure iced orange Curaçao
few drops iced cassis

1 Pour the grappa slowly round one side of a well-
chilled shot glass.
2 Gently pour the Chartreuse round the other side.
3 Pour the Curaçao gently into the middle and add a
few drops of cassis just before serving. Don't stir.
Drink slowly!

tornado

If these liquors are really well iced, you will certainly create a tornado in your glass when you pour one into the other – just sit and watch them swirling for a moment!

Serves : 1

1 measure peach or other favourite schnapps, frozen

1 measure black Sambuca, frozen

1 Pour the schnapps into an iced shot glass.
2 Then gently pour on the Sambuca over the back of a spoon.
3 Leave it for a few minutes to settle and separate before you down it.

anouchka

Sambuca is liquorice flavoured and therefore not to everyone's taste. However, used here with a dash of blackberry liqueur and a measure of iced vodka, it's a great combination.

Serves : 1
1 measure vodka, iced
dash black Sambuca
dash crème de mure
a few blackberries

1 Pour the vodka into a chilled shot glass.
2 Add a dash of the Sambuca and then a dash of the crème de mure.
3 Dress with a few blackberries, fresh or frozen.

silverberry

This drink is perfect for one of those very special occasions – except that you really can't drink very many!

Serves : 1
1 measure raspberry vodka, iced
1 measure crème de cassis. iced
1 measure Cointreau, iced
edible silver paper or a frozen berry

1 Carefully and slowly layer the three liquors in the order listed, in a well-iced shot glass or tall thin cocktail or elgin glass.
2 They must be well iced first and may need time to settle into their layers.
3 Dress with the silver paper or a frozen berry.

peachfloyd

Shots of this look stunning in the right type of glass, but as they are for drinking down in one, keep them small and have everything really well chilled.

Serves : 1

1 measure peach schnapps, chilled
1 measure vodka, chilled
1 measure white cranberry and peach juice, chilled
1 measure cranberry juice, chilled

1 Stir all the ingredients together over ice and pour into an iced shot glass.

chillywilly

Truly a cocktail for the brave-hearted – the heat depends on the type of chilli (some are much more fiery than others) as well as the quantity you add and whether the chilli was deseeded first. For an even spicier cocktail, use chilli vodka as well!

Serves : 1
2 measures vodka
1 tsp chopped fresh chilli
cracked ice cubes

1 Shake the vodka over ice with the chilli until a frost forms.
2 Strain into a small chilled tumbler.

dandy

The fruit flavour added at the end is what gives this rich combination a special touch.

Serves : 1
½ **measure rye whisky**
½ **measure Dubonnet**
dash Angostura bitters
3 dashes cassis
ice
few frozen berries

1 Mix the first four ingredients with ice and strain into an iced shot glass.
2 Dress with a berry or two.

napoleon'snightcap

Instead of hot chocolate at bedtime, Napoleon apparently favoured a chocolate-laced brandy with a hint of banana. Daring and extravagant!

Serves : 1

1¼ measures cognac
1 measure dark crème de cacao
¼ measure crème de banane
1 tbsp cream

1 Stir the first three ingredients in a mixing glass with ice.
2 Strain into a chilled cocktail glass and spoon on a layer of cream.

whitediamond**frappé**

This is a crazy combination of liqueurs, but it works well once you've added the lemon. The extra crushed ice at the last minute brings out all the separate flavours.

Serves : 1
¼ measure peppermint schnapps
¼ measure white crème de cacao
¼ measure anise liqueur
¼ measure lemon juice
ice

1 Shake all the ingredients over ice until frosted.
2 Strain into a chilled cocktail glass and add a small spoonful of crushed ice.

starsand**swirls**

You will need a steady hand for this one – preferably two pairs of steady hands.

Serves : 1
1 measure Malibu
½ measure strawberry or raspberry liqueur
1 tsp blue Curaçao
ice

1 Chill a small shot glass really well.
2 Pour in the Malibu and add a large ice cube.
3 Carefully pour in the other two liqueurs from opposite sides of the glass very slowly so they fall down the sides and swirl around.

nuclearfallout

This is similar to a pousse-café, where the liqueurs are layered, but, in this case, the heaviest liqueur is coldest and is added last, to create the slow sinking effect!

Serves : 1

1 tsp raspberry syrup
¼ measure of maraschino
¼ measure of yellow Chartreuse
¼ measure Cointreau
½ measure well-iced blue Curaçao

1 Chill all the liqueurs, but specifically put the blue Curaçao in the coldest part of the freezer. Also chill a shot, pousse-café or elgin glass.

2 Carefully pour the first four ingredients one by one in layers over the back of a teaspoon.

3 Finally, pour in the blue Curaçao and wait for the fallout!

non-alcoholic cocktails

Young and old will enjoy this collection of alcohol free cocktails. Perfect for a hot summer's day (or the designated drivers amongst you), these tasty drinks are brimming with health-giving ingredients.

orangeand**lime**iced**tea**

Iced tea is always refreshing and, even if you are not a keen tea drinker, this version is especially fresh and fruity. Keep some in the refrigerator if you don't use it all up.

Serves : 2

300ml/10 fl oz freshly brewed tea, cooled

100ml/3½ fl oz orange juice

4 tbsp lime juice

1–2 tbsp brown sugar

wedges of lime

granulated sugar

8 ice cubes

slices of fresh orange, lemon or lime

1 When the tea has chilled, add the orange juice, lime juice and sugar to taste.

2 Take two glasses and rub the rims with a wedge of lime, then dip them in granulated sugar to frost.

3 Fill the glasses with ice cubes and pour on the tea.

4 Dress with slices of fresh orange, lemon or lime.

fuzzypeg

A child's delight both in taste and its incredibly strange colour! It could be made with other drinks too.

Serves : 1
2 scoops vanilla ice cream
1 measure lime juice cordial
cola
ice

1 Blend the ice cream and lime cordial together for 5-10 seconds with a little cola.
2 Pour into a tall glass filled with ice and top up with cola.
3 Drink through straws.

berryberry**red**

This combination is delicious with fresh or frozen raspberries, so you can make this cocktail all year round. Cut down on the meringue if you find it a little too sweet.

Serves : 1
50g/2oz raspberries
4 measures cranberry and raspberry juice
crushed ice
1 small meringue, crumbled
blackberry-flavoured sparkling water

1 Set aside a couple of attractive berries for decoration
2 In a blender, whizz the rest of the fruit with the juice and crushed ice.
3 Put half the meringue in the base of a chilled tall glass, pour on the fruit slush and top up with the water.
4 Dress with raspberries and the remaining crumbled meringue.

pineapplesmoothie

This is a popular combination for a
smoothie – one smooth sweet fruit and
one tangy and textured fruit. You
might like to try your own variation.

Serves : 2
125ml/4 fl oz pineapple juice
juice of 1 lemon
100ml/3½ fl oz water
3 tbsp brown sugar
175ml/6 fl oz natural yoghurt
1 peach, cut into chunks and frozen
100g/4oz frozen pineapple chunks
wedges of fresh pineapple

1 Blend all the ingredients, except the pineapple
wedges, in a food processor until smooth.
2 Pour into glasses and dress the rims with wedges of
fresh pineapple.

tropicaldelight

A velvety-smooth, delicately scented drink without alcohol. This can be served at any time of day – and it's delicious for breakfast.

Serves : 4
2 large ripe mangoes
1 tbsp icing sugar
600ml/1 pint coconut milk
5 ice cubes
flaked toasted coconut

1 Peel the mangoes, coarsely chop the flesh and discard the stones.
2 Place the flesh in a blender with the sugar and blend until completely smooth.
3 Add the coconut milk and ice to the blender and process until frothy.
4 Pour into 4 tall glasses and sprinkle with flaked toasted coconut to serve.

spicybanana**shake**

Banana blends well even when partly frozen and it tends to create a luxuriously thick finished drink.

Serves : 2
300ml/10 fl oz milk
½ tsp mixed spice
150g/5oz banana ice cream
2 bananas, sliced and frozen

1 Blend the milk in a food processor with the mixed spice, the banana ice cream and half the frozen banana.
2 Add the remaining banana gradually and process until well blended.
3 Pour into tall iced glasses and drink with straws.

carrotchill

Carrots have a really sweet flavour, especially very young raw carrots. The juice makes a great combination with the peppery watercress.

Serves : 2
500ml/17 fl oz carrot juice
30g/1oz watercress
1 tbsp lemon juice
sprigs of fresh watercress

1 Pour the carrot juice into a blender.
2 Add the watercress and lemon juice and process until smooth.
3 Transfer to a jug, cover with film and chill in the refrigerator for at least an hour,
4 When thoroughly chilled, pour into glasses and dress with sprigs of fresh watercress. Serve at once.

cherrykiss

A refreshing and almost calorie-free cocktail, perfect for dieting or simply for one of those non-alcohol occasions.

Serves : 2
8 ice cubes, crushed
2 tbsp cherry syrup
500ml/17 fl oz sparkling water
2–3 splashes fresh lime juice
maraschino cherries on cocktail sticks

1 Divide the crushed ice between two glasses and pour the syrup over.
2 Add the lime juice and top up with sparkling water.
3 Decorate with the maraschino cherries on cocktail sticks and serve.

cranberryenergise

Packed with vitamin C and many other
vitamins, this will really wake you up
and leave you bursting with energy.

Serves : 2
300ml/10 fl oz cranberry juice
100ml/3½ fl oz orange juice
150g/5oz fresh raspberries
1 tbsp lemon juice
slices of lemon or orange and twists of peel

1 Pour the cranberry juice and orange juice into a food
   processor and process gently until combined.
2 Add the raspberries and lemon juice and process
   until smooth.
3 Pour the mixture into glasses and decorate with slices
   or twists of fresh lemon or orange. Serve immediately

fauxkir

A non-alcoholic version of the classic wine cocktail, this drink is just as colourful and tasty. French and Italian fruit syrups are often the best quality and have the most flavour.

Serves : 1

1 measure chilled raspberry syrup
chilled white grape juice

1 Pour the raspberry syrup into a chilled wine glass.
2 Top up with the grape juice.
3 Stir well to mix.

berrycream

This is pure fruit blended to a perfectly smooth cream but with no wicked cholesterol added! So you can enjoy some luxury, knowing it is also very healthy.

Serves : 2
350ml/12 fl oz orange juice
1 banana, sliced and frozen
450g/1lb frozen forest fruits (such as blueberries, raspberries and blackberries)
slices of fresh strawberry

1 Pour the orange juice into a food processor.
2 Add the banana and half of the forest fruits and process until smooth.
3 Add the remaining forest fruits and process until smooth.
4 Pour the mixture into tall glasses and decorate the rims with slices of fresh strawberry.
5 Add straws and serve.

memorylane

Hedgerow pickers will have many happy memories of freshly crushed blackberry or elderberry drinks. This version needs no trips to the hedge, just a few berries from the shops and some fresh citrus. Very healthy and refreshing.

Serves : 1
a few blackberries or blackcurrants
1 tbsp caster sugar or to taste
juice ½ lemon
juice ½ lime
crushed ice
lemonade or fruit sparkling water

1 Reserve a few berries for garnish. Place the remaining fruit in a chilled tumbler with sugar and crush or stir until well mashed.
2 Add crushed ice and the fruit juice and top up with lemonade to taste.
3 Top with the reserved whole berries.

pinkpussy**foot**

This is just as delicious made with raspberries and framboise liqueur.

Serves : 1
1 measure lemon juice
1 measure orange juice
2–3 strawberries, mashed
1 measure fraise
½ egg yolk
dash grenadine
ice
slice of strawberry

1 Shake all the ingredients really well together.
2 Pour into a cocktail glass and finish with a slice of strawberry.

mimi

This is a delicious mix without the kick
of the vodka, so make a batch for non-
alcohol drinkers and add the vodka for
yourself!

Serves : 1
2 measures pineapple juice
½ measure coconut cream
crushed ice
2 measures vodka (optional)
slice or fan of fresh pineapple

1 Whizz the first three (or four) ingredients in a blende
for a few seconds until frothy.
2 Pour into a chilled cocktail glass and finish with a
piece of pineapple.

raspberrylemonade

If you like real old-fashioned lemonade,
then you will love this version.

Serves : 4
2 lemons
100g/4oz caster sugar
100g/4oz fresh raspberries
few drops vanilla essence
crushed ice
sparkling water, iced
sprigs of lemon balm

1 Trim the ends off the lemons, scoop out and chop
   the flesh and place in a blender with the sugar,
   raspberries, vanilla and ice.
2 Blend for 2–3 minutes or until there are no lumps.
3 Strain into tall glasses and top up with ice cubes and
   water. Finish with sprigs of lemon balm.

juicyjulep

Taken from the Arabic word, which in turn was derived from Persian, meaning rose water, it seems likely that julep was always a non-alcoholic drink until imaginative bourbon-drinking Derby-goers hijacked the term.

Serves : 1

1 measure orange juice
1 measure pineapple juice
1 measure lime juice
½ measure raspberry syrup
4 crushed fresh mint leaves
cracked ice cubes
ginger ale
fresh sprig of mint

1 Shake the orange juice, pineapple juice, lime juice and raspberry syrup with the mint leaves vigorously over ice until well frosted.

2 Strain into a chilled Collins glass, top up with ginger ale and stir gently.

3 Dress with a sprig of fresh mint.

lemonfizz

A refreshing summer fizz to enjoy with
no effort – keep some in the refrigerator
ready to top up at the last minute.

Serves : 1
2 fresh lemons
crushed ice
peel of half a lemon
1 tbsp sugar
lemonade, iced

1 Squeeze the fresh lemons and pour the juice into a
chilled highball glass filled with crushed ice.
2 Add the piece of peel and sugar to taste and stir
briefly. Add lemonade to taste.

applesour

The lemon and lime juice give this cocktail more than a hint of sharpness, but it is soon masked by the sweet honey and apple flavours.

Serves : 1
4 measures pure apple juice
juice of 1 lemon and 1 lime
1 measure sugar syrup or clear honey
1 small egg white
crushed ice
4–5 raspberries
long strip apple peel

1 Whizz all ingredientsm except the fruit and peel, in a blender until very frothy and partly frozen.
2 Put three raspberries in the base of an iced tall glass, crush with a wooden spoon and then pour in the fruit slush.
3 Dress with the raspberries and a strip of peel.